Kevin McCormack

Western Branches, Western Byways

Ian Allan
PUBLISHING

First published 2013

ISBN 978 0 7110 3764 9

Published by Ian Allan Publishing Ltd, Hersham, Surrey KT12 4RG.

Printed in Bulgaria

Visit the Ian Allan Publishing website at *www.ianallanpublishing.com*

FRONT COVER Two years to go before closure and the weeds are beginning to take hold as neglected 2-6-0 Mogul No 6345 calls at Wiveliscombe on its way from Barnstaple to Taunton during the summer of 1964. *Allan S. Clayton/Online Transport Archive*

REAR COVER Heading into the mists of time, 0-4-2 tank No 1458 works the 'Chalford Flyer' on the final day of services, 31 October 1964. This, and the concurrent withdrawal of the Berkeley Road–Sharpness service, was expected to mark the end of WR auto-train working, but it didn't! *Author*

PAGE 1 A typical South Wales valleys train of empty coal wagons is seen at Maesycwmmer Junction on 3 May 1964 hauled by 0-6-2 tank No 5659. Maesycwmmer, near Hengoed, was well known for the magnificent viaduct built to carry the Taff Vale Extension Railway over the Rhymney Valley and is now used as a cycle route. *Alan Sainty collection*

Introduction

This colour album, *Western Branches, Western Byways*, covers a lost world of secondary services comprising branches and other non-main line activity, both local passenger and freight operations, as seen in the 1950s and 1960s.

All BR regions had their fair share of minor lines and much of the charm which they exuded, particularly those in rural areas, was not confined to the WR: pretty station buildings, well-kept flower beds on the platforms (tended by smart-looking staff, often with little else to do), pride in the job, a community spirit etc – and the occasional train! Many of these lines had auto-trains ('push and pulls') enabling the driver to operate the locomotive from the end vestibule of the carriage (trailer) when the train was being propelled, with the fireman remaining on the footplate (and sometimes unofficially driving the train, as I found out when I cadged a ride in the auto trailer vestibule of the Tiverton Junction-Tiverton train and wondered, as we were being propelled, why the driver spent the whole journey chatting to me instead of operating the controls!).

While other regions also used auto-trains, it was the antique-looking motive power which gave WR branches a particular quaintness. This had much to do with the Collett '14XX' 0-4-2 tanks or 'Fourteeners' as we called them. The 75 members of this class were hardly old, being built between 1932 and 1936. The Southern Region was still operating branch line services into the 1960s with Victorian locomotives. However, little attempt was made by the Great Western Railway (GWR) to make the 'Fourteeners' look significantly different from the locomotives they replaced, mainly updated members of the Armstrong '517' class built between 1868 and 1885. The similarity in appearance was further reinforced in 1946 when the Collett '14XX' tanks lost their original 48XX numbers to make way for oil-burning 2-8-0s, taking on a number series previously occupied by later batches of 517s. Indeed, this series had only just been vacated in time because No 1436 was not withdrawn until November 1944 and No 1442 (not the one in Tiverton Museum!) survived until May 1945.

The 'Fourteeners' were a successful class, being economical to operate and having fast acceleration. Withdrawals started in February 1956 as steam push and pull work diminished but the final survivors lasted until May 1965. Four are preserved, including one (No 1420) which had the honour of hauling a Royal Train when HM The Queen visited Abingdon in 1956. However, WR auto-trains were not confined to haulage by '14XX' 0-4-2s. There were auto-fitted 0-6-0 pannier tanks of the '54XX' and '64XX' classes and even some auto-fitted '55XX' 2-6-2 tanks. Nevertheless, it was undoubtedly the sight of the archaic-looking 0-4-2 tanks normally attached to a single trailer that made them so adorable, prompting the locals to give these trains pet names such as the 'Marlow Donkey', 'Tivvy Bumper' (Tiverton branch), 'Chalford Flyer', 'Wallingford Bunk' and 'Bulliver' (Ashburton branch).

The images of WR branches and secondary routes in this book reflect scenes that have vanished from the national rail network. Of course, some BR lines did escape closure and are still operating today and others have been reopened in recent years as rail travel increases. Sadly though, it is rare to find original station buildings and other ex-GWR infrastructure still in place. The relentless pursuit of economies has meant that local stations are mainly unstaffed halts with bus shelter-type structures on the platforms.

Dr Beeching is inevitably blamed for the axing of branch and secondary lines but some of this criticism is unfair. As Chairman of the British Railways Board from 1961-65, he was told by the Government of the day to find ways of making the railways profitable. His controversial report, 'The Reshaping of British Railways – Part 1', was published on 27 March 1963, recommending the closure of almost one-third of the rail network and more than half of all railway stations. However, this was against the background of one-third of route miles generating just 1% of passenger traffic (and a Minister of Transport who had a particular interest in motorway development).

In reality, more lines were shut before the 'Beeching Axe' than were shut as a result. Following nationalisation of the railways in 1948, a branch line committee of the newly-formed British Transport Commission had been charged with the task of shutting down the least used branch lines and 3,318 miles of railway were closed between 1948 and 1962. This still left a rail network which was too large and in many cases unsustainable but time has shown that the Beeching cuts were too quick and too deep. Greater effort to introduce economies in staffing and signalling, and earlier recognition of the valuable social service they provided, could have saved some doomed lines. And ironically, even with his axe, Beeching was unable to return the railways to profitability.

Yet all is not lost. There are numerous preserved lines which enable us to enjoy the delights of Western branches and byways,

transporting us back to those halcyon days. And the inspiration for standard gauge railway preservation – volunteers running a full-sized passenger-carrying railway? Arguably, it was T. E. B. Clarke. He was the scriptwriter of the Ealing Comedy film, *The Titfield Thunderbolt*, filmed in 1952. Influenced by the successful operation of the narrow-gauge Talyllyn Railway which was saved by volunteers in 1951 following the death of its owner, Sir Henry Haydn Jones in 1950, T. E. B. Clarke saw no reason why local people should not operate a full-sized railway line closed by BR and duly wrote the Titfield Thunderbolt story. Three locomotives were used in the film, two of which were 0-4-2 tanks Nos 1401 and 1462. However, it took a further eight years or so before fiction became fact, with the opening of the Bluebell Railway in Sussex in August 1960.

In this book, it has not been possible to include photographs of all WR branches and secondary lines for a variety of reasons. The emphasis has been on portraying services which are no longer operated, using colour material of acceptable quality (which often rules out pictures taken on dull days and on dodgy film) and, wherever possible, featuring less well known, but identifiable locations. Also, it is hoped that the photographs in this book will be new to readers. I have attempted to arrange material in geographical groups but, with many lines crossing over county boundaries, the allocation is somewhat arbitrary. An index of locations can be found on page 96 which may be of help.

Finally, I am very grateful to the various sources from which I have drawn material. The majority of pictures have been provided by the Online Transport Archive, a charity which acts as a repository for collections donated or bequeathed by photographers. Other contributors that I must thank are Alan Sainty (for original material from his collection), Bob Bridger (for use of Charles Firminger's and Peter Bunde's photographs and for other assistance), Nick Lera, Neil Davenport, the LRTA (Light Railway Transit Association (London Branch)) and Frank Dumbleton. A few of the images are my own, taken from age 13 upwards.

Kevin R. McCormack
Ashtead, Surrey
April 2013

West Drayton & Yiewsley station, some 13 miles from Paddington on the West of England mainline, was the junction for branches to Uxbridge (Vine Street) and Staines West (simply called Staines until 1949), on which ex-GWR diesel railcars from Southall shed were frequently used until diesel multiple-units (DMUs) took over. This photograph, taken around 1960, depicts one of the later, angular railcars, W24W, dating from 1940 and withdrawn in October 1962, standing at Cowley, the only intermediate station on the Uxbridge branch. This line, only some two miles long, opened in 1856 but a request by Cowley villagers for their own station was dismissed at that time. The GWR relented in 1904, probably motivated by the competition it faced from the Underground which reached Uxbridge in that year (with the inaugural train being hauled by Met No1, star of the Underground 150th Anniversary celebrations in 2013!). In 1907, the GWR opened another branch to Uxbridge, this time from the Birmingham line at Denham, which terminated at Uxbridge (High Street) station with the prospect, never realised, of being extended across the town to join up with the West Drayton branch. With Uxbridge then possessing three railway stations serving three different routes, the West Drayton branch station was renamed Uxbridge (Vine Street) in 1907. However, Underground services were always more popular, especially for commuting to London, and the WR branches eventually closed, passenger services on the West Drayton branch being withdrawn on 10 September 1962. *Harry Luff/Online Transport Archive*

The last bastion of auto-train operation in the London area was the Maidenhead/Bourne End/Marlow line which is still open today. DMUs took over following the last day of steam on Sunday 8 July 1962 (when a truncated service operated from Marlow to Cookham due to engineering works at the Maidenhead end). Until 1961, the 'Marlow Donkey', as it was affectionately known, also made some journeys beyond Bourne End over the now defunct section through Wooburn Green and Loudwater to High Wycombe, terminating in a bay platform there. The line from Maidenhead to High Wycombe was completed in August 1854 and formed part of a through line to Oxford (reached in 1864) via Princes Risborough, taking eight miles off the route from London to Oxford via Didcot. The branch from Bourne End (originally called Marlow Road) to Marlow (initially named Great Marlow) opened on 28 June 1873. This view shows 0-4-2 tank No 1438, attached to its auto-trailer (so it has not been shunting wagons to form a mixed train, which happened sometimes), and taking water opposite the station platform at Marlow. *Alan Sainty collection*

No 1421 seemingly threads its way around houses at Furze Platt Halt as it hauls the 3.42pm from Marlow to Maidenhead on 5 March 1961. Furze Platt Halt opened on 5 July 1937 to serve the growing community in this area on the northern outskirts of Maidenhead. The station name was shortened to Furze Platt on 5 May 1969. *Charles Firminger*

The author, who dragged his mother along for the steam-hauled 'Marlow Donkey's' last day, had taken along a large union flag to add to the decorations on the locomotive and found there were none (and duly got her to hide the flag!). He had expected similar treatment, as seen here, to that bestowed upon No 1440 on the last day of steam operation three weeks earlier on the Princes Risborough–Aylesbury branch. *Author*

The motive power for the Princes Risborough to Aylesbury auto-trains in latter years varied between '14XX' 0-4-2s, '64XX' panniers and the large wheeled '54XX' class (with 5ft 2in in wheels instead of 4ft 7¾in. On 12 March 1961 the auto-train was in the hands of No 5420, a locomotive very familiar to the author as having been one of the regular engines on the Ealing Broadway–Greenford push and pull service. Here it is leaving Monks Risborough and Whiteleaf Halt with the 10.35am from Aylesbury to Princes Risborough. On the last day of steam auto-trains, Sunday 17 June 1962, 0-4-2 tank No 1440 was used and, as seen on the previous page, the locomotive crew had taken the trouble to decorate their engine. The author and a companion, who had travelled to Princes Risborough from Ealing Broadway via Maidenhead and High Wycombe, had clearly not studied the Sunday timetable. We were waiting on the up platform which served Aylesbury wondering why there was a crowd of people on the down platform. Luckily, we joined the throng just in time to see the Aylesbury auto-train propel itself into Princes Risborough from High Wycombe and, having climbed aboard, were then astonished to find ourselves stranded at Aylesbury as No 1440 shunted its auto trailer, W220W Thrush, and prepared to return 'light engine'. Fortunately, the crew took pity on these two hapless schoolboys and gave us a cab ride back to Princes Risborough, dropping us at the top of an embankment on the approach to the station, out of sight of the signalman! *Alan Sainty collection*

The Watlington branch from Princes Risborough opened in 1872 following the abandonment in 1868 of plans to join it up with the Cholsey to Wallingford line which had opened two years earlier. The terminus at Watlington suffered, like so many others, from being located some distance from the habitation it was meant to serve, resulting in the line not being well patronised in its latter days. Passenger services were withdrawn on 1 July 1957 and goods traffic beyond Chinnor ceased from 2 January 1961. Freight trains serving a cement factory at Chinnor continued, the last such movement taking place on 20 December 1989. On 3 April 1960 a railtour using 0-4-2 tank No 1473 visited the branch and is seen at Chinnor. Subsequently demolished, this station has now been beautifully recreated by the Chinnor and Princes Risborough Railway Preservation Society which has been operating train services over part of the original line since 1994. *Charles Firminger*

ABOVE The Princes Risborough to Oxford line via Thame opened in 1864, this being the final section of the route from Paddington to Oxford which, as stated on page 5, was eight miles shorter than the journey via Didcot. However, the line to Oxford via Didcot became the established route and the Princes Risborough to Oxford line became merely a branch. By the 1930s it was suffering from competition from bus services and consequently additional halts with only basic facilities were added to attract more passengers. One of these was Towersey Halt which was opened on 5 June 1933, where one of Oxford shed's '61XX' large prairie tanks was photographed on 14 June 1962. *Nick Lera*

RIGHT The author travelled on the final day of passenger services on 6 January 1963 when No 6111 was used. The train had to contend with deep snow, typified in this view of an elderly passenger trudging along the platform at Horspath Halt for the last time. *Author*

The hollyhocks and roses are blooming on 30 July 1958 as the so-called 'Wallingford Bunk', comprising 0-4-2 tank No 1407 and its auto trailer, rests at Wallingford station before heading for Cholsey & Moulsford. The branch opened in 1866 and was meant to continue to Benson and Watlington but this extension never materialised (see page 8) and Wallingford remained the terminus of the branch, making its length only some 2.5 miles. The junction station was Wallingford Road which was renamed Moulsford when the branch opened. In 1892, the station was moved closer to Cholsey and became Cholsey & Moulsford, and is now plain Cholsey. Passenger services to Wallingford ceased on 13 June 1959 and the branch terminus was demolished in 1969, the site having being severed from the remainder of the line by a new road. On the left of the photograph is the branch engine shed. *Charles Firminger*

Two years after passenger services were withdrawn the branch became active again following the construction of a malt plant (distillery) alongside the railway at Wallingford. Freight services then operated for the next 20 years until the owners switched to road transport. The malt plant closed in 1999 and was demolished in 2004. However, the distillery secured the branch's retention, enabling the Cholsey & Wallingford Preservation Society to take over the line in 1981. Back in 1968, BR allowed the Great Western Society to operate auto-trains over the branch on two occasions, on 15 April and 21 September, the latter event breaking the steam embargo as a result of advance publicity having been issued about the services before the ban was announced. This view taken on the earlier date shows 0-4-2 tank No 1466 and auto trailer No 231 standing alongside the malt plant, nicknamed Wallingford Cathedral. *Author*

Encroaching into Gloucestershire was the 22-mile-long Fairford branch from Oxford, which had originally been built in two stages. The first section was built by the Witney Railway Company to join that manufacturing town with the GWR line at Yarnton and thence to Oxford, this part opening in 1861. The second section was opened in 1873 by the East Gloucestershire Railway Company whose ambition was to reach Cirencester and join up with the Midland & South Western Junction Railway, thereby reaching Cheltenham. The line never went beyond a field in Fairford but the intention to extend was the reason for that station not being built as a terminus. Passenger services ended on 16 June 1962 but the branch remained open as far as Witney for freight until 2 November 1970. Only one station building remains intact today, Carterton, which qualifies as one of the strangest to be found on the GWR. Opened on 2 October 1944 to serve RAF Brize Norton, it looked like a typical military structure and was made out of concrete blocks with an extraordinary awning made of asbestos sheeting and old rails. Following closure, the building has served as a pig sty, a store for farm machinery and, following the addition of rustic cladding in 1980, now as riding stables, complete with that awning! The signalbox beyond the platform end has been acquired by the Swindon & Cricklade Railway. The photographs on these pages depict pannier tank No 7412 on arrival at Fairford with the 12.15pm from Oxford on 10 January 1959, Carterton station viewed from the same train on that date and No 7404 near Eynsham with the 4.26pm from Oxford to Fairford on 24 February 1962. *Charles Firminger - all*

This view of the western end of Newbury station looking north has, on the down side, 'City' class 4-4-0 No 3440 *City of Truro* waiting in the Whitchurch/Winchester Chesil bay while a pannier tank simmers in the Lambourn Valley bay on the up side.
City of Truro, the first engine to attain at least 100mph, entered service in 1903, being the 2000th locomotive to be built at Swindon Works. The locomotive was renumbered 3717 in 1912, a few months after its appearance had been altered by acquiring an extended smokebox following the fitting of a superheater, and was withdrawn in 1931, being subsequently preserved. It was restored to working order in 1957 and allocated to Didcot shed from where, in between hauling specials, it was often used on the Didcot, Newbury & Southampton line. The Didcot to Newbury section had opened in 1882 and reached a dead end at

Winchester in 1885, extended in 1881, GWR trains then operating over London & South Western Railway (LSWR) lines to Southampton. The route south of Newbury was closed to normal passenger traffic on 7 March 1960 and the last day of passenger services north of Newbury was 8 September 1962. Meanwhile, *City of Truro* was withdrawn for the second time in its life in 1961. Newbury was also the starting point for the 12-mile branch to Lambourn. This opened on 2 January 1898, with the last regular passenger trains running on 4 January 1960, although freight operations continued as far as Welford Park until 1973. These two views of Reading-based 'Flying Banana' No W16W at Newbury and Lambourn stations were taken in 1953. W16W entered service in April 1936 and was withdrawn in November 1957. *Harry Luff/Online Transport Archive; Frank Hunt/LRTA - two*

An LSWR lamp standard and a GWR bench are indicative of the joint use of Weymouth Town station, the WR presence being further represented by No 4947 *Nanhoran Hall* about to depart with the 3.10pm stopping service to Bristol on 10 April 1960. Adjacent to Weymouth station was Melcombe Regis station, on the Weymouth and Portland Railway, the proximity of these stations facilitating the transfer of passengers. Melcombe Regis was last used for branch passenger trains on 1 March 1952. However, it continued in operation for several years as an overflow annexe to Weymouth station. The Weymouth & Portland Railway had opened in 1865 and was jointly operated by the GWR and LSWR. It was one of three separate railways on the island, the others being an Admiralty (military) line and the Easton & Church Hope Railway (E&CHR), which also became a joint GWR/LSWR line, thereby creating a single branch. The E&CHR opened to freight in 1900 but passenger services were delayed until 1902 due to the Admiralty link between the two railways being deemed sub-standard. In these views, pannier tank No 4624 stands at Melcombe Regis with a railtour on 8 July 1956 and is then seen at Easton station. The station building is the stone edifice in the centre of the picture and the pile of rubble on the left is the remains of the engine shed and signalbox. *Charles Firminger; John McCann/Online Transport Archive - two*

FACING PAGE References to railways at Weymouth would be incomplete without mention of the Quay line. Latterly, three members of the '1366' class of six outside-cylindered dock shunters had been shedded at Weymouth for use on this branch until displaced by diesels in 1962. No 1369 is the only survivor and is preserved on the South Devon Railway. Here it is threading its way through the traffic and then shunting at the harbour on 10 April 1960. *Charles Firminger - both*

ABOVE On 1 January 1963, regional boundary changes occurred, resulting in WR auto-trains being introduced on the following two former Southern Region (SR) branches, Seaton Junction-Seaton in Devon and Yeovil Junction-Yeovil Town in Somerset, both having previously been worked by elderly, ex-LSWR 'M7' 0-4-4 tanks. The Seaton branch opened in 1868 with two intermediate stations, Colyton and Colyford. WR auto-trains using '64XX' panniers allocated to Exmouth Junction operated from March–November 1963, when DMUs took over workings until closure on 7 March 1966. However, a temporary shortage of these units saw 0-4-2 tank No 1442 and an auto trailer hastily drafted in to work the Seaton branch for a few weeks in February/March 1965. This view of Colyton station depicts No 6430, now preserved. Dating from 1937, the engine is fortunate to have been saved because it was withdrawn in October 1964 and sold to a scrap merchant and was then repurchased by the Dart Valley Railway as a source of spares for the other two preserved class members, Nos 6412 and 6435. Now returned to operational condition No 6430 can normally be found on the Llangollen Railway. Colyton station has also survived, becoming the northern terminus of the 2ft 9in gauge Seaton Tramway. *Alan Sainty collection*

Honoured with three railway stations, Yeovil was in both LSWR and GWR territory, the former company using Yeovil Junction on the London-Exeter main line, the GWR operating from Yeovil Pen Mill on the Castle Cary-Weymouth line and both companies using the now defunct Town station. This was closed to passengers on 3 October 1966 when the Junction shuttle was withdrawn and ironically was the most centrally located of the stations. During the period of WR auto-train working which began in March 1963, 0-4-2 tank No 1451 is seen propelling its auto trailer out of Yeovil Town station towards Yeovil Junction on 20 October 1963. Take a close look at the locomotive and see how much prettier it looks compared with the majority of '14XX' members featured in this book! It doesn't have the ugly top feed box behind the chimney - a fitting which was introduced on this class from 1944. Its purpose was to pre-heat and de-aerate the boiler feed water in order to improve boiler efficiency and reduce damage, but a few 'Fourteeners' managed to end their service life carrying boilers without top feed including No 1451 which was not withdrawn until July 1964. *Alan Sainty collection*

Heathfield in Devon was the junction for the Teign Valley line to Exeter and for the Moretonhampstead branch from Newton Abbot. The latter branch opened in 1866 and the Teign Valley line opened in 1882, although it was not extended to Exeter until 1903. Passenger services on the Teign Valley line were withdrawn on 9 June 1958 and the last public passenger service on the Moretonhampstead branch ran on 28 February 1959. These two pictures were taken on a freezing 25 January 1958; the first depicts large prairie 2-6-2 tank No 4117 arriving at Heathfield with the 10.10am from Moretonhampstead; the second depicts the station nameboard, which is suffering from a lack of commas, and lists stops on the Teign Valley line but omits reference to the Moretonhampstead branch.
Charles Firminger - both

Small prairie 2-6-2 tank No 5536 waits in the bay platform at Heathfield with a Teign Valley train on 25 January 1958. Our intrepid photographer then made the journey to Moretonhampstead behind 0-4-2 tank No 1472 where the train was duly photographed at the terminus ready for the return journey, after the locomotive had run round its non-auto-fitted carriages.

Charles Firminger – both

The attractive Totnes to Ashburton line opened in 1872 and the branch train came to be nicknamed 'Bulliver' by the locals. However, the line was never profitable, the last scheduled passenger train operating on 3 November 1958 and freight services, which had always been the mainstay of the branch, being withdrawn on 7 September 1962. Most of the line was subsequently preserved as the Dart Valley Railway (now the South Devon Railway) and was officially opened by a certain Dr Beeching (!) on 21 May 1969. Regular passenger services, however, were never operated beyond Buckfastleigh because the trackbed to Ashburton was required for widening the A38 road. Fortunately, the Brunel station building with its all-over roof is listed and survives as a garage, and the goods shed is also still extant. These photographs show No 1472 (again) at the distinctive Ashburton terminus on 21 June 1958 and the station

nameboard at Totnes, on the West of England mainline, photographed on 25 January 1958.

Alan Sainty collection; Charles Firminger

The Launceston branch from Plymouth was completed in 1865 and closed to passenger services on 31 December 1962, although a small section at the southern end of the line has since been preserved by the Plym Valley Railway. The station before Launceston was Lifton, where small prairie 2-6-2 tank No 5564 was photographed. Another intermediate station, Yelverton, was the junction for the Princetown branch which traversed the desolate terrain of Dartmoor and was notable for its sharp curves and steep gradients to which the 11-strong '44XX' class of even smaller prairie 2-6-2 tanks with their 4ft 1½ in driving wheels (6in smaller in diameter than those of the similar '45xx' locomotives) were particularly well suited. The branch closed on 3 March 1956, this view at Princetown being taken some three years earlier. *Alan Sainty collection; Peter Bunde*

The Liskeard & Looe Railway opened in 1860 from Moorswater, beneath the GWR main line, where it connected with the Liskeard & Caradon Railway. Initially a mineral railway, the branch opened to passengers in 1879 but was not well used due to the remoteness of Moorswater from Liskeard. In 1901, a steep curve was created to bring the branch up to the level of the mainline at Liskeard and a separate station, at right angles to the main line station, was built (see page 96). The line was taken over by the GWR in 1909 and remains open today, being reprieved from closure at the last minute in 1966. Small prairie tank No 4569 stands at Looe station (since resited) in September 1959 and the proximity of the platform to the East Looe River estuary was a source of fascination to the young author when he travelled behind No 5539 on 22 July 1961.

Alan Sainty collection; Author

Newquay was served by branches from Truro and from Par, the former line closing to passengers in February 1963. The latter line was opened to passengers in 1876, originally as a direct route from Fowey to Newquay via Par, and is flourishing today as the Atlantic Coast Line. Indeed, as well as being served by local trains and used for china clay freight operations, it even has some direct trains to Plymouth and Paddington, although whether it does High Speed Trains (HSTs) any good crawling at 20mph along the branch is another matter! On 27 April 1961, resplendent small prairie 2-6-2 tank No 5544 was photographed waiting to leave Par on a Newquay service. When the author travelled on the line in late July 1961, he found himself in a timewarp created by the sight of a locomotive in GWR livery at Newquay and an elderly clerestory-roofed camping coach at one of the intermediate stations, Luxulyan. Pannier tank No 9635 was constructed at Swindon by the GWR in 1946 and had therefore never been repainted in 15 years. Camping coach W9906W was built in 1902 as a first/second corridor composite previously numbered (7)472 and was converted in 1952.

Alan Sainty collection; Author - two

6245 W

CAMPING COACH

The Fowey branch train headed by 0-4-2 tank No 1419 stands at Lostwithiel. This station, on the Cornish mainline, is still open today but the Fowey line was closed to passengers on 4 January 1965. The branch had originally been built in 1869, 10 years after Lostwithiel station opened, in order to move goods and iron ore from Restormel Iron Mine to Fowey harbour for onward transportation by boat. Unfortunately for the branch's owners, a rival company opened a line from Par to Fowey in 1874 and, with decreasing freight traffic, the Fowey branch was closed six years later, only to reopen, this time for both goods and passenger traffic, in 1895. The line from Par to Fowey closed in 1968 while the branch to Lostwithiel has reverted to its original role as a freight-only line, transporting china clay in large hopper wagons, as opposed to the small tarpaulin-covered open trucks visible behind No 1419.

Harry Luff/Online Transport Archive

Photographed on 18 June 1958, small prairie tank No 4552 shunts at Lansalson, terminus of the Trenance Valley Branch, which was built exclusively for china clay traffic and never had a passenger service. Opening in 1910 and closing in 1968, the branch left the Cornwall main line about a quarter of a mile west of St Austell. Moving deeper into Cornwall we come to the St Ives branch from St Erth, now called the St Ives Bay Line, another line proposed for closure and then reprieved. When the branch opened in 1877, it was the last broad gauge passenger line to be built, being converted to standard gauge when the broad gauge was abolished in 1892. This view of the branch train at St Ives station headed by a '45xx' 2-6-2 tank dates from 1953 but the terminus looks nothing like this today, having been re-sited and modernised. *Alan Sainty collection; Peter Bunde*

FACING PAGE TOP The Taunton–Barnstaple line via Dulverton was a hilly route across Somerset and Devon some 45 miles long which opened in 1873 and carried its last passengers on 3 October 1966. The GWR station, latterly known as Barnstaple Victoria Road, was closed to passengers on 12 June 1960 from which date trains from Taunton terminated at the SR's Barnstaple Junction station. This is where 2-6-0 Mogul No 6327 was photographed on 15 July 1963 after hauling the 1.15pm from Taunton. The locomotive is pulling the empty stock forward, passing Bulleid Pacific No 34106 *Lydford* in the process, prior to detaching itself from the train in order to use the turntable before returning to Taunton. *Charles Firminger*

FACING PAGE BOTTOM Dulverton was roughly half-way between Taunton and Barnstaple and was the junction for the Exe Valley line from Exeter via Tiverton. On leaving Exeter, the GWR branch split from the LSWR line at Cowley Bridge Junction, where this shot was taken. 0-4-2 tank No 1442 (since preserved) hurries the 3.25pm from Exeter St Davids to Dulverton on 12 January 1963. *Charles Firminger*

ABOVE The Exe Valley branch opened in its entirety in 1885 and was closed to passengers on 7 October 1963. In this view of Dulverton on 11 June 1962, a Barnstaple train stands in the main platform, connecting with the auto-train from Exeter hauled by 0-4-2 tank No 1434. *Alan Sainty collection*

LEFT The principal station between Exeter and Dulverton was Tiverton and this photograph taken there features Exeter shed's only two 0-4-2 tanks noted by the author to be still wearing black livery in August 1962 (the others seen were in lined green). Behind the water column is No 1462 working an Exe Valley train to Dulverton while in the foreground, and unusually in the west side bay platform, is No 1466 (now preserved at Didcot) on a Tiverton Junction service. For many, the sight of two 'Fourteeners' on trains in adjacent platforms would have been good enough but the author wanted three! This was possible at certain times of the day at Tiverton station (achievable by Exe Valley trains crossing in the station standing alongside the Tiverton Junction service and because the 'Fourteeners' always faced northwards). Unfortunately, the only time the author was there to witness this event during his week-long stay in Tiverton was on a very dull, wet day which, due to his primitive camera, precluded photography. Whenever the weather was good, non-auto pannier No 3659 would haul one of the Exe Valley trains and therefore spoil the party! *Author*

ABOVE The Tiverton Junction–Tiverton branch opened as early as 1848, with Tiverton being a terminus station until the completion of what became the Exe Valley line in 1885, when the station was rebuilt. The branch service was nicknamed the 'Tivvy Bumper' and is commemorated in Tiverton Museum, not by a mere model train, but by a life size exhibit, 0-4-2 tank No 1442! Following its withdrawal in May 1965 (becoming the last of its class, along with No 1450, also preserved), No 1442 (featured on page 30) was purchased by Viscount Amory and steamed to Tiverton with invited guests in October 1965, whereupon it was temporarily mounted on a plinth opposite the station before being placed in the museum. Tiverton station was closed to passengers on 5 October 1964 when the 'Tivvy Bumper' was withdrawn, the Exe Valley services having already been withdrawn one year previously, on 7 October 1963. Freight services were withdrawn on 5 June 1967. This view shows No 1405 in the eastern side bay platform working the 8.40am to Tiverton Junction on 4 June 1958, three months before the engine's withdrawal. *Alan Sainty collection*

ABOVE The mainline station, Tiverton Junction, closed on 12 May 1986, by which time it had long since ceased to be the junction for the Tiverton branch and also for the legendary Culm Valley light railway, otherwise known as the Hemyock branch. This line was notable for its mixed trains and for using a gas-lit passenger coach. The branch opened in 1876 and was closed to passengers on 7 September 1963, remaining open for the movement of milk wagons until the creamery at Hemyock closed on 31 October 1975. The sharp curves on the line necessitated the use of short wheelbase stock, thus eliminating auto trailers, and speeds were too slow to charge batteries for electrically-lit carriages and risked breaking the dynamo belts. Two ex-Barry Railway coaches (one in operation and the other kept as a spare) were latterly used until 1962 when they were replaced by Eastern Region Thompson-designed four-compartment brake seconds. The idyllic charm of parts of this line is encapsulated in this view of 0-4-2 tank No 1468 shunting milk wagons at Hemyock.
R. W. A. Jones/Online Transport Archive

FACING PAGE Other aspects of the Hemyock branch were less scenic as portrayed in these views of No 1468 at Coldharbour Halt (opened on 23 February 1929 to serve the adjacent textile mill) and No 1471 preparing to leave Hemyock on 18 June 1960 (a less idyllic view with the creamery in the background).
R. W. A. Jones/Online Transport Archive; Charles Firminger

This view epitomises the decline of the former SR/London Midland Region (LMR)-operated Somerset & Dorset Joint Railway (S&D) once the WR assumed responsibility for the northern part of the line from Templecombe to Bath in 1958, including the Highbridge branch, and the remainder of the line from 1 January 1963. The Highbridge branch had been opened in 1856 to provide Glastonbury, a significant manufacturing town, with a coastal connection for shipment of goods. The line ran from Evercreech Junction, on the main S&D route from Bath to Bournemouth, to Highbridge and Burnham. One of the intermediate stations was Edington Junction which underwent several name changes. Opening as Edington Road, the name was changed to Edington Junction in 1890 when the line to Bridgwater opened and a second platform added. This line then closed to passengers in December 1952 and, with the station consequently ceasing to be a junction, it was renamed Edington Burtle on 8 June 1953. '2251' class 0-6-0 No 3216 stands in the surviving platform in August 1963 while the train guard and a female passenger stand silhouetted against the desolate backdrop. Passenger services were withdrawn on 7 March 1966 when the entire S&D was shut down.

Martin Jenkins/Online Transport Archive

Yatton, on the Bristol–Bridgwater–Taunton mainline, was the junction for two branches. One was to Wells and Witham (the Cheddar Valley line) which closed to passengers in 1963, from which there was a branch to Blagdon (closed to passengers in 1932). The second was to Clevedon which terminated adjacent to the station of the former Weston, Clevedon & Portishead Railway. The Yatton to Clevedon line opened in 1847 and, unusually, was closed for freight over three years before passenger services were withdrawn on 3 October 1966. By this time, DMUs had taken over but, as pictured here on 28 April 1957, the branch train was in the hands of 0-4-2 tank No 1454. Ironically, Yatton station had opened in 1841 as Clevedon Road, and now the station nameboard proclaims 'Yatton for Clevedon', because, being only 3.5 miles away, it is now the closest railway station to Clevedon! *John McCann/Online Transport Archive*

The Midland Railway's Berkeley Road to Sharpness branch was built to serve the docks on the Severn Estuary at Sharpness, opening to freight in 1875 and to passengers a year later. On the opposite side of the estuary, the Severn Bridge Railway was simultaneously constructing a line at Lydney Town in the Forest of Dean to connect with the Severn & Wye Valley Railway and the GWR at Lydney Junction, and then via a river bridge across the Severn to join the Sharpness branch from Berkeley Road. This through route was opened in 1879 and became a GWR/Midland Railway Joint line in 1894. All was well until 25 October 1960 when the Severn Bridge was wrecked in a tragic collision in fog by two tanker barges. This resulted in services from Berkeley Road having to terminate at Sharpness instead of Lydney Town. The branch had already been singled by then and it closed to passengers on 2 November 1964. This view of pannier tank No 6437 was taken at the only intermediate station, Berkeley. Occasional freight trains still serve Sharpness Docks and a heritage railway in this area has been proposed. Meanwhile, the Dean Forest Railway has reopened Lydney Junction station and built a new Lydney Town station. *Alan Sainty collection*

The celebrated Chalford auto service operated along part of the Gloucester to Swindon line (the so-called Golden Valley line, not to be confused with the Golden Valley Railway in Herefordshire which ran between Pontrilas and Hay-on-Wye). The line opened in its entirety in 1845 with just a few intermediate stations but was transformed when the GWR introduced its first 'rail motor' service on 12 October 1903 between Stonehouse and Chalford (later extended to Gloucester) in order to serve the growing communities and industry in the Stroud Valley. The existing stops north of Chalford which were created in 1845 (Stonehouse, Stroud and Brimscombe) and in 1897 (Chalford itself) were augmented by four new halts in 1903, a further two shortly after, and a final one in 1930. Auto-trains replaced the rail motors as traffic increased but the decline of local industry and greater car ownership heralded closure, the last day of passenger services being 31 October 1964. Earlier that year 0-4-2 tank No 1472, no longer with top feed apparatus (see picture on page 23), is seen at Brimscombe Bridge Halt on its way back to Gloucester. This halt was unusual in not having facing platforms, the Chalford platform being located on the other side of the overbridge. *Nick Lera*

The Golden Valley line lives up to its name as a 'Chalford Flyer' approaches Chalford station on 31 October 1964 headed by auto-fitted pannier No 6412, this locomotive sharing last day honours with No 1458. The service is believed to have earned its nickname because of the eight-mile sprint between Gloucester and Standish Junction when the auto-trains ran alongside the Midland line to Bristol and are reputed to have reached speeds of up to 70mph by overtaking the main line trains! Unsurprisingly, the auto-trains were packed on 31 October 1964 and, remarkably, one of the passengers on the final day was Harold Gubbins who had been a fireman on the first day, 12 October 1903. No 6412, which dates from 1934, was withdrawn from Gloucester shed immediately after the cessation of the Chalford auto-trains and was purchased for preservation, being currently owned by the South Devon Railway. *Author*

No 1458 stops at Bowbridge Crossing Halt on 31 October 1964 as it propels a Chalford auto-train to Gloucester. The self-powered rail motors (carriages containing vertical steam boilers) on these services were victims of their own success through the number of passengers they were attracting because they were hard pushed to tow or propel a loaded auto trailer unless the line was relatively level. The Golden Valley line was uphill all the way from Gloucester to Chalford and indeed Brimscombe was at the foot of Sapperton bank which reached 1 in 70 at Chalford. Passenger numbers also increased through the GWR operating from 9 January 1905 local area road motor (bus) services from Stroud which linked up with the trains. Ninety-nine steam rail motors were built but problems with their being underpowered and normally having to be kept in engine sheds, making it hard to keep the passenger accommodation clean, saw their withdrawal between 1915 and 1935 and replacement by more flexible auto-trains. The vertical boilers were removed and the passenger accommodation extended, turning them into normal auto trailers. The sole surviving converted vehicle, trailer No 212, has been restored by the Great Western Society and, complete with new vertical boiler, has assumed its original identity as rail motor No 93, operating on the national rail network in November 2012 on the Liskeard-Looe branch (see page 96).
Author

LEFT The Chalford service's normal clientele wait for a Gloucester-bound auto-train at Downfield Crossing Halt while enthusiasts hang out of a Chalford-bound train hauled by No 1458 on the last day of services. Sometimes an auto-fitted locomotive was not available, as on 7 September 1964 when large prairie tank No 6122 was photographed at Stroud paired with an auto trailer, requiring the engine to 'run round' at Chalford. *Author; Marcus Eavis/Online Transport Archive*

ABOVE '2251' class 0-6-0 No 2287 stands at Lydbrook Junction in the Forest of Dean in summer 1964. The station was on the Ross-on-Wye-Monmouth (Troy) line which opened in 1873 and closed to passengers on 5 January 1959. The section from Lydbrook Junction to Ross remained open to freight until 1965, latterly just serving a wire factory (as evidenced by the cable drums in the picture). The station had been a junction for the Severn & Wye Railway from 1875 until passenger services north of Lydney Town were withdrawn in 1929, ending the passage of through trains to Lydbrook Junction from the Sharpness branch via the Severn Bridge, all of which then terminated at Lydney Town. *Alan Sainty collection*

FACING PAGE The Forest of Dean in Gloucestershire had a complex network of tramways and railways to bring the Forest's timber, coal and other minerals to the outside world. Passenger traffic was always sparse and generally short-lived, the carrying of freight being the main activity. These two photographs depict the final days of steam working in the Forest of Dean. Deep amongst the ferns pannier tank No 4698 shunts at the ochre mine on the Sling branch on 18 August 1965. This short branch, which opened in 1876 and closed on 2 January 1967, replaced a tramway and climbed sharply after leaving the Coleford to Parkend section of the former Midland Railway/GWR Severn & Wye Joint Railway at Milkwall station. A section of this latter railway, from Lydney Junction to Parkend, has been preserved by the Dean Forest

Railway. Another pannier, No 3675, brings a freight bound for Northern United Colliery out of Bradley Hill tunnel, Upper Soudley, on 11 October 1965. The building, which still stands, is the former gatekeeper's cottage, built to GWR design, and housed the railwayman responsible for the crossing and for handing out/collecting the single-line token for passage through the tunnel. *W. Potter, courtesy of Martin Jenkins/Online Transport Archive - both*

ABOVE Sharing a platform at Monmouth (Troy) are a Chepstow-bound auto-train headed by pannier tank No 6439 standing in front of a Ross-on-Wye auto-train with a '14XX' 0-4-2 tank in charge. More details of Monmouth (Troy) and its services can be found overleaf. *R. W. A. Jones/Online Transport Archive*

FACING PAGE Monmouth (Troy), called Monmouth Troy House from its opening in 1857 until 1904, was formerly a through station for passenger trains operated by four different railway companies, the destinations being Pontypool, Ross-on-Wye, Coleford and Chepstow. Passenger services to Coleford ceased as early as 1917 and when services to Pontypool were withdrawn in June 1955, Monmouth (Troy) effectively became a terminus. Passenger trains to Ross-on-Wye and Chepstow (the latter being the Wye Valley line) were withdrawn on 5 January 1959 and the station building was subsequently dismantled and re-erected at Winchcombe on the preserved Gloucestershire Warwickshire Railway. Freight services continued until

6 January 1964 and are illustrated here by pannier tank No 7789 shunting at Monmouth (Troy) on 1 November 1958 and an unidentified pannier tank, having just left the station, hauling a light goods train over the Chepstow line bridge across the River Wye, with the bridge to Ross-on-Wye visible in the background. *Charles Firminger; R. W. A. Jones/Online Transport Archive*

ABOVE Heading a Hereford-Gloucester train in September 1964, two months before this line closed to passengers, large prairie 2-6-2 tank No 4107 pulls away from the little-used station at Ballingham, situated between Holme Lacy and Fawley stations. *Alan Sainty collection*

Ross-on-Wye, the location of these photographs, opened in 1855 as an intermediate station on the Hereford, Ross and Gloucester Railway. It was also the terminus of a branch from Monmouth (Troy) which was usually worked by a '14XX' 0-4-2 tank and auto-trailer (see page 45). This branch closed to passengers on 5 January 1959 but Ross-on-Wye remained open to passengers until Hereford-Gloucester services were withdrawn on 2 November 1964 and for freight until 1 November 1965. The main station building was demolished but has been used as the pattern for the preserved Severn Valley Railway's Kidderminster station.

ABOVE AND FACING PAGE TOP On 1 November 1958, Mogul 2-6-0 No 6353 is seen entering the station with the 10.25am Hereford-Gloucester and another Mogul, No 6395, is pictured on the same day waiting to leave with the 9.40am Gloucester-Hereford train. No 6395 is still carrying black livery and is representing the period when the only green locomotives were express passenger ones whereas No 6353 has benefited from the subsequent enlightened WR policy of applying lined green livery to all passenger classes.

FACING PAGE BOTTOM By contrast, the appalling external appearance of No 7815 *Fritwell Manor*, as it prepares to leave with the 10.25am Hereford-Gloucester on 5 September 1964, typifies the state of the steam fleet during this later period.
Charles Firminger - two; Marcus Eavis/Online Transport Archive

'2251' class 0-6-0 No 2242 hauls a Hereford-Gloucester train over Backney Bridge, between Fawley (not the one with an oil refinery and power station!) and Ross-on-Wye, in September 1964. The bridge has since been demolished and only the stone supports remain. Near the bridge was Backney Halt, a later additional stop on the line, being opened in 1933 and shutting in 1962, two years before the line was closed to passengers. The '2251' class was designed by C. B. Collett as an updated version of the '2301' class of 0-6-0s (better known as 'Dean Goods'), and consisted of 120 engines built between 1930 and 1948, using the numbers 2200-2299 and 3200-3219. The type started at number 2251 because the last members of the '2221' class ('County Tanks') still occupied some numbers from 2221 to 2250 when construction of the '2251' class began. Only one member has escaped scrapping: No 3205 built in 1946 and based on the South Devon Railway. *Alan Sainty collection*

In 1873, the Ross & Ledbury Railway was authorised to build a line between these towns via Dymock but abandoned the scheme and instead joined forces with the Newent Railway which had approval to build a line from Ledbury to Gloucester through Dymock. The railway, which came to be known as the Daffodil line, opened in 1885 and closed to passengers on 13 July 1959. These photographs date from July 1957 and show GWR diesel railcars at the delightful stations of Dymock (upper) and Newent (lower).
R. W. A. Jones/Online Transport Archive - both

ABOVE Pannier tank No 4614 waits at Ashchurch with an Evesham train on 1 June 1963. The main line from Birmingham to Bristol went through the middle of the station with two branches located on each side, one to Tewkesbury, Upton-upon-Severn and Malvern and the other to Evesham and onward to Alcester and Redditch. The last surviving sections of these branches serving Ashchurch were closed to passengers on 14 August 1961 and 17 June 1963 respectively and Ashchurch station itself, by then renamed Ashchurch for Tewkesbury, was closed on 15 November 1971, only to reopen on 1 June 1997, but without the attractive, original station buildings which had been demolished in 1972. The other views show No 4614 again, this time at Beckford Station on 29 May 1963 (*above right*) and No 3745 at Evesham Midland station on 25 May 1963 (*below right*). *W. Potter, courtesy Martin Jenkins/Online Transport Archive - all*

FACING PAGE Most of the line closures in the 1950s and 1960s involved country stations and halts but there were also some more significant casualties such as Wolverhampton Low Level and Dudley. The two stations were closed to passengers in 1972 and 1964 respectively but the services illustrated here, linking Wolverhampton, Dudley and Stourbridge Junction over part of the erstwhile Oxford, Worcester & Wolverhampton Railway, ceased on 30 July 1962. These views taken on 2 June 1962 show large prairie tank No 4179 firstly at Wolverhampton Low level with the 12.25pm to Stourbridge Junction and then at Dudley.

ABOVE The last station on this line before Stourbridge Junction was Brettell Lane, just north of which was Kingswinford Junction, giving access to the Wombourne/Kingswinford Branch which connected with the Shrewsbury to Wolverhampton line at Oxley Junction. The branch opened in 1925 and closed to passengers just seven years later. The section between Tettenhall and Kingswinford closed to freight on 24 June1965. Remarkably clean pannier tank No 4696 pulls a freight train off the branch at Kingswinford Junction, in the presence of another pannier, No 3605 and a diesel shunter, on 2 June 1965. However, pride of place must surely go to the magnificent gas lamp!
Charles Firminger - all

ABOVE Bewdley, now the HQ of the heritage Severn Valley Railway operating between Kidderminster and Bridgnorth, was once a busy junction. The station was served by trains from three directions, north/south from Shrewsbury to Hartlebury via Bridgnorth, east from Kidderminster and west from Woofferton and Tenbury Wells. Passenger trains were withdrawn on the Tenbury line on 1 August 1962, between Shrewsbury and Bewdley on 9 September 1963 and between Kidderminster, Bewdley and Hartlebury on 5 January 1970. In this view Mogul 2-6-0 No 6388 brings a freight into Bewdley on 9 July 1959, portraying a scene which is hardly any different today. *Alan Sainty collection*

FACING PAGE These photographs depict GWR diesel railcars operating between Kidderminster/Bewdley and Tenbury Wells/ Wooferton and were taken at Bewdley and Wyre Forest. On this particular occasion, the railcar made an unexpected stop in the middle of nowhere whereupon two men carrying several small sacks boarded the train and distributed the contents to the crew and various passengers. Something dodgy appeared to be happening and the two railway enthusiasts on board were viewed with suspicion as they were carrying cameras! They concluded that the boarding party were poachers and that the railcar had made a pre-arranged unofficial stop. *Alan Sainty collection; E. C. Bennett or Martin Jenkins/Online Transport Archive*

Cleobury Mortimer was a station between Wyre Forest and Neen Sollars on the Kidderminster/Bewdley to Tenbury Wells/Woofferton line, much of which straddled the Shropshire/Worcestershire border. The branch from Bewdley westwards was built in two stages. The Woofferton & Tenbury Railway opened in 1861 and the Tenbury & Bewdley Railway opened three years later. In 1908, Cleobury Mortimer became a junction with the construction of the Cleobury, Mortimer & Ditton Priors Light Railway. Passenger services ceased on that railway on 26 September 1938 and the line closed completely on 11 September 1939, only to reopen for goods traffic in June 1941 following the establishment of a Royal Navy Armaments Depot at Ditton Priors, the branch remaining in use until 16 April 1965. It is visible behind the station nameboard in this photograph taken on 18 July 1960 of a GWR diesel railcar in early DMU livery with 'speed whiskers' on its way to Woofferton. *Neil Davenport*

Woofferton, a junction station, is a hive of activity in this scene depicting GWR diesel railcar No W28W in the platform which has probably arrived from Kidderminster and Bewdley. Woofferton was on the former joint GWR/LNWR Shrewsbury & Hereford Railway which eventually provided a through route from Crewe to Abergavenny and Newport (the north and west route through the Welsh Marches). This line is still open but Woofferton station is closed although the main station building and goods shed survive and are used for commercial purposes. Woofferton was also served by auto-trains on the Shrewsbury-Hereford line which ran between Ludlow and Leominster, sometimes nipping over to Tenbury Wells when they reached Woofferton (this latter section of line closed to passengers on 31 July 1961). GWR diesel railcars were introduced on many local branches in this area in an attempt to make these lines economically more viable but the increase in private car ownership usually meant this was to no avail. Three diesel railcars survive: streamlined No 4 at Steam Museum, Swindon, and angular cars No 20 on the Kent & East Sussex Railway and No 22 which is operational at Didcot Railway Centre. *Alan Sainty collection*

Until the absorption of the Welsh railway companies into the GWR in 1922 the Taff Vale Railway was one of the train operators in the Cardiff area and valleys and was noted for its decorative architecture, represented here by the signalbox, footbridge and station building at Lavernock. This station was on the Cadoxton branch, a coastal spur providing a passenger service between Penarth and Barry until 8 May 1968. DMUs replaced 0-6-2 tanks such as No 5693 in 1958. Cadoxton was a junction on the former Barry Railway to Llantwit Major and Bridgend (the Vale of Glamorgan line). The first station west of Barry was Rhoose and this is how it looked on 19 April 1958. Closed in June 1964, it re-opened in June 2005 but has been totally transformed and rebadged as Rhoose Cardiff International Airport, the longest station name on national rail! *R. W. A. Jones/Online Transport Archive; Charles Firminger*

Some 12 miles west of Cardiff on the mainline to Swansea lay Llantrisant which was once a junction served by three separate railway companies. It even had an engine shed which, as late as 1959, still housed 16 steam locomotives. The shed shut in October 1964 and the station closed on 2 November 1964. However, after an interval of nearly 30 years, the station has been rebuilt, reopened and renamed Pontyclun but it is a pale shadow of its former self and is now described officially as 'an unstaffed minor railway station'. One of the branches leading from Llantrisant was the Ely Valley line to Blaen-Clydach. This was primarily a mineral line but passenger services were introduced as far as Pen-y-Craig in 1901, being withdrawn on 9 June 1958. Shortly before closure, immaculate 0-4-2 tank No 1471, coupled to a GWR Collett auto trailer, stands ready to depart at Llantrisant. *R. W. A. Jones/Online Transport Archive*

Another line from Llantrisant was one acquired by the Taff Vale Railway which ran to Cowbridge (the northern section) and later extended to Aberthaw (the southern section) where there was a lime works and a small harbour on the Bristol Channel. The Vale of Glamorgan line from Barry to Bridgend also passed through Aberthaw (indeed the coal traffic serving Aberthaw Power Station was later to save the Vale line from being lifted when it initially closed in June 1964) but the respective railway stations were at different levels and a long walk away. Traffic was sparse, particularly on the southern section which was closed to passengers in 1930 and to freight two years later. The northern section, with intermediate stations at Llanharry and Ystradowen, survived somewhat longer, with passenger services lasting until 26 November 1951 and freight services continuing until the Llanharry iron works closed in 1976. On 13 July 1957, No 1471 again, but this time wearing its previous plain black livery, was used on a railtour hauling two Collett auto trailers and is seen here at Cowbridge. *R. W. A. Jones/Online Transport Archive*

Pannier tank No 6419 stands at Porthcawl with an auto-train to Pyle, on the Cardiff-Swansea mainline, shortly before closure of the branch to passengers on 9 September 1963. It remained open for freight until 1 February 1965. The line originated as the Dyffryn, Llynfi & Porthcawl Railway which built a horse-drawn tramway in 1829 to transport coal and iron ore from the Llynfi Valley through Tondu and Pyle to the harbour at Porthcawl. In 1834, a further horse-drawn tramway to take minerals to Porthcawl was built from Bridgend to Pyle. These tramways merged in 1846, becoming the Llynvi Valley Railway. Another railway, the Ogmore Valley Railway, opened in 1865 to join Nantymoel with Porthcawl and in the following year the two railway companies amalgamated to form the Llynvi & Ogmore Railway. The GWR absorbed the railway in 1883. As well as being on the Cardiff-Swansea mainline Bridgend was also served by the Vale of Glamorgan line from Cardiff via Llantwit Major. In addition, trains ran via Tondu and Maesteg to Abergwynfi on

the Llynvi Railway Extension. The station nameboard at Bridgend, photographed on 19 April 1958, is strong on history but is of limited use to non-locals who want a train to Porthcawl or Nantymoel! *Alan Sainty collection; Charles Firminger)*

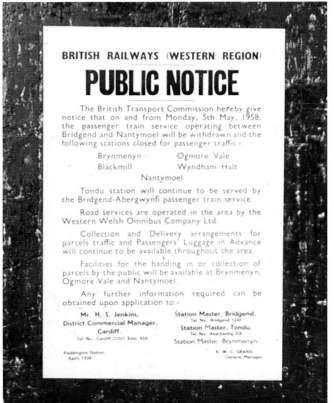

Pannier tank No 7753 waits to leave Nantymoel with the 4.40pm to Bridgend on 19 April 1958, three weeks before passenger services were withdrawn (the closure notice at Bridgend says it all). Nantymoel, situated in the Ogmore valley, is a former mining village, the last pit having closed in 1983. The branch opened on 1 August 1865 to provide access to the high quality coal in the area. The last passenger train ran on 3 May 1958. *Charles Firminger - both*

The Llynfi & Ogmore Railway (L&OR) built an extension from Tywith (later renamed Nantyffyllon) into the Afan valley. This started in 1875 with the building of a tunnel at Caerau, known as the Maesteg tunnel, which was completed in 1877 (but at the cost of 13 lives). The GWR had an agreement with the L&OR to operate and manage the line and opened up its own colliery to extract steam coal, construction starting in 1877 with Sir Daniel Gooch, the GWR's Chairman, cutting the first sod.

The line as far as Cymmer was opened to passengers on 16 July 1880 and services to the terminus at Abergynfi commenced on 22 March 1886. Three years earlier, on 1 July 1883, the GWR had absorbed the L&OR. On 18 April 1960, pannier tank No 9609 is depicted arriving at Abergynfi with a train from Tondu. Passenger services were withdrawn just a few weeks later, on 13 June 1960, but mineral traffic continued until 1969.
Alan Sainty collection

ABOVE AND FACING PAGE The topography of the South Wales valleys involved many challenges when the railways were built and required many tunnels and bridges. Walnut Tree viaduct at Taffs Well (Radyr) was one of several spectacular structures. The Barry Railway built this viaduct over the River Taff valley in order to provide a direct link between Barry Docks and the Merthyr valley through Penrhos Lower Junction and Llanbradach. Always a freight only line, the section north of Penrhos was dismantled in 1937 and the southern end was closed in 1963 following a signalbox fire, leaving a short section over Walnut Tree viaduct accessed from Penrhos Lower Junction in order to serve the Steetley Dolomite limestone quarry located immediately above the southern end of the viaduct. These freight trains ceased in 1967 and the viaduct was dismantled between 1969 and 1974, although one pier has been preserved as a landmark and a second pier and an abutment also survive. These scenes depict (above) 0-6-2 tank No 5632 leaving Taffs Well on the Taff Vale Railway's Cardiff-Merthyr line with Walnut Tree viaduct in the background, (facing page top) Hawksworth pannier No 9446 viewed from the guard's van of a freight train crossing the viaduct in April 1965 and (facing page bottom) No 9446 shunting wagons in the dolomite quarry, with one of the stone caps of the viaduct just visible on the extreme right of the picture. *R. W. A. Jones/Online Transport Archive - all*

It is hard to imagine that this was once a bustling station served by over 20 trains a day! Situated on the Morlais Junction to Merthyr line which was jointly operated by the Brecon & Merthyr Railway (B&M) and the LNWR, the station opened in 1868 as Pontsarn & Vaynor, was renamed Pontsarn Halt in 1953 and closed in 1961. The existing hut had once stood alongside a more substantial building which was subsequently demolished, leaving the hole in the ground visible on the left of the picture. This melancholy scene dates from 4 November 1961, exactly one week before the last passenger train ran, and depicts auto-fitted pannier tank No 6433 on the 10.02am from Pontsticill Junction to Merthyr. Much of the trackbed of this short, scenic line has been converted into the Taff Trail footpath and Cardiff to Brecon cycleway. Fortunately, the two splendid viaducts over which the trains on this line used to pass, one at Pontsarn itself and the other at Cefn Coed, can still be enjoyed. *Charles Firminger*

On 27 September 1963 0-6-2 tank No 6622 brings a Neath to Pontypool Road train across the highest railway viaduct in Britain and the third highest in the world (until its demolition). This is the spectacular Crumlin Viaduct, the least expensive bridge of its size ever constructed, which spanned the valleys of Ebbw and Kendon as well as the Newport to Ebbw Vale railway line. This latter route was closed to passengers on 30 April 1962 and reopened on 6 February 2008 but there is no chance of restoring services on the high level line. The last scheduled passenger service on the viaduct was a Pontypool to Treherbert train on 13 June 1964 and dismantling of this remarkable wrought iron lattice structure commenced two years later.

Designed to withstand the high winds prevalent in the valleys, the viaduct had opened in 1857, being part of the Taff Vale Extension project linking the Newport, Abergavenny & Hereford Railway at Coed-y-Gric North Junction, Pontypool, with the Taff Vale Railway and GWR at Quakers Yard. The Extension line provided an east/west route for mineral trains as an alternative to the numerous north/south routes from the pit heads in the valleys to the docks at Cardiff and Newport. It also provided access to LNWR-controlled lines without the need for the freight trains to take a roundabout route via Cardiff and Newport in order to reach other parts of Britain. *W. Potter, courtesy Martin Jenkins/Online Transport Archive*

ABOVE 2-8-0 tank No 5206 hauls a long train of empty wagons through Aberbeeg, which was the junction for lines to Ebbw Vale and to Brynmawr, on 18 June 1959. This locomotive had a long service life, being completed in June 1923 and withdrawn in May 1965. *R. W. A. Jones/Online Transport Archive*

FACING PAGE TOP The introduction of diesel multiple-units on Welsh Valley lines commenced on 13 January 1958. The aim was to create operating savings and increase passenger loadings through modernity and increased comfort in an attempt to save the lines from closure, although in most cases this was to no avail. This scene dating from 7 May 1960 at Blaenavon Low Level depicts a DMU with 'speed whiskers'. Blaenavon boasted two railway stations: High Level and Low Level. The first to close to passengers was the former LNWR (and latterly GWR)

High Level station on the Pontypool–Brynmawr line in 1941. The WR Low Level station, providing services to Newport via Pontypool Road (Crane Street), closed on 30 April 1962. Part of the ex-LNWR route is now preserved and operated by the Pontypool & Blaenavon Railway, whose current southern terminus is the site of the former Blaenavon High Level station. *Charles Firminger*

FACING PAGE BOTTOM Quakers Yard station at Edwardsville also had two levels and this view shows 0-6-2 tank No 5615 hauling a freight through the Low Level station on 6 October 1962. This station was opened by the Taff Vale Railway in 1858 and is currently served by trains operating between Abercynon and Merthyr Tydfil but the attractive platform building has sadly been demolished. *Charles Firminger*

LEFT Exiled to the former Vale of Neath Railway from the London division, large prairie tank No 6144 takes on water at Quakers Yard High Level while working the 3.50pm from Aberdare High Level to Pontypool Road on 11 April 1964. This line closed a few weeks later on 15 June.
Charles Firminger

BELOW Large prairie tank No 4157 brings the 2.25pm Pontypool Road-Neath into Treharris on 11 April 1964. This station also closed when services were withdrawn on 15 June 1964 and, as at Quakers Yard High Level, the tracks removed.
Charles Firminger

RIGHT Nelson & Llancaiach was a junction for the Taff Vale Railway's Neath to Pontypool Road line and the Rhymney Railway/GWR Taff Bargoed Joint Railway to Dowlais. The station was another to close on 15 June 1964 and some two months earlier, on 11 April, 0-6-2 tank No 5677 was photographed entering the station with the 12.37pm Ystrad Mynach–Dowlais (Cae Harris) train. Instead of the five tracks in this picture, there is just one today, which is used for freight traffic. *Charles Firminger*

LEFT Like the other stations on these two pages Penrhiwceiber closed in 1964 but now here's the difference: it reopened in 1988! Located on the Aberdare Branch of the Merthyr Line between Abercynon and Mountain Ash, 2-8-2 tank No 7222 passes this basic, former Taff Vale Railway station on 11 April 1964. *Charles Firminger*

Pannier tank No 7439 calls at Abergwili (spelt Abergwilli until 1893) on its journey from Carmarthen to Llandilo (now spelt Llandeilo). This branch was built by the Llanelly Railway & Dock Company (which was subsequently absorbed by the LNWR) to join up with that company's Central Wales Line (now marketed as the Heart of Wales Line) from Swansea to Shrewsbury. The Llandilo line branched off the Carmarthen-Aberystwyth line at Abergwili Junction and Abergwili was the first station after Carmarthen. Abergwili station opened on 1 June 1865 and closed when passenger services ended on 9 September 1963. The Gwili Railway, a heritage operation, runs trains over part of the now closed Carmarthen-Aberystwyth line and intends to extend southwards to a new station called Carmarthen North on the site of Abergwili Junction. *Alan Sainty collection*

Clarbeston Road, between Whitland and Fishguard, was a typical 'Road' station situated in the middle of nowhere which was not particularly close to the village it was named after, yet its arrival created its own village called, you've guessed it, Clarbeston Road! The station used to be quite busy, being the junction for branches to Neyland/Milford Haven and to Fishguard as well as being served by boat trains and local services. It is now an unstaffed request stop. In this view from 1958, pannier tank No 5713 is taking water at Clarbeston Road after bringing a two-coached train from Fishguard Harbour into the bay platform to connect with a train to Paddington. The locomotive represents the earlier type of '57XX' pannier tank with narrower cab favoured, after withdrawal from BR, by London Transport to replace its elderly fleet of steam locomotives and which, unlike the later panniers, were suitable for the limited clearances in underground tunnels. *Alan Sainty collection*

Noted for its severe gradients, tight curves and rural nature, the Whitland-Cardigan branch was completed in 1886 after various setbacks, construction having started back in 1870. Cardigan was a popular destination for holiday makers but, outside the holiday season, passenger traffic was generally sparse, with little patronage obtained from the nine intermediate stations. Luckily, the volume of freight traffic helped considerably in sustaining the line but the heavy staffing requirements (there were seven level crossings) and the slow speed of the trains (some averaged as little as 15mph) made the branch an obvious candidate for closure. The last passenger service ran on 8 September 1962 and freight services were withdrawn on 27 May 1963, after which the track was lifted. These views depict small prairie tank No 4557 on arrival at Cardigan with a mixed train consisting of a Syphon G van and a single carriage on 30 August 1962 and, on its way to the terminus with the same train, at Llanglydwen. Finally, on a different occasion, pannier tank No 1613 is seen leaving Kilgerran, the last station before Cardigan, on a train from Whitland. *John McCann/Online Transport Archive - two; R. W. A. Jones/Online Transport Archive*

ABOVE Pannier tank No 9602 stands at Fishguard Harbour, an important gateway to Ireland, in September 1962. This station, which is owned by Stena Line, opened in 1906 when the Clarbeston Road and Letterton Railway was built, all sailings to Ireland from West Wales having previously used the port at Neyland. This port rather than Fishguard had been chosen because it avoided the need to build the section from Clarbeston Road to Fishguard which had been authorised in 1845 but which was not proceeded with at that time due to doubts about the volume of traffic to and from Ireland. This was due to the terrible Irish Potato Famine which lasted from 1848 to 1852 and caused enormous loss of life and mass migration. *Alan Sainty collection*

FACING PAGE These photographs depict the Aberystwyth to Carmarthen line which opened fully in 1867 and was closed due to flooding in December 1964 between Aberystwyth and Strata Florida, with the southern end closing to passengers on 22 February 1965. However, this latter section remained open to freight until 1973. On 9 August 1963, Standard Class 4 2-6-4 tank No 80101 was working the 5.40pm Aberystwyth-Carmarthen and took on water at Strata Florida. When the train reached Lampeter it was intercepted by pannier tank No 7407 with two milk wagons, intent on hitching a lift. The ensuing mixed train is seen climbing near Bryn Teify on its way to Carmarthen. *Charles Firminger - both*

It is June 1971 and this must surely be the final steam train to visit Craig-y-Nos on the former Neath & Brecon Railway, this station being the last, travelling south, before Colbren Junction, where the Neath and Swansea lines split. Partly funded by Adelina Patti, the world-renowned opera singer who lived in nearby Craig-y-Nos Castle, the railway station was equipped with a lavish private waiting room for her use and was linked to the castle by a private road. Passenger services were withdrawn on 15 October 1962 but freight traffic serving the adjacent Penwyllt quarry continued until the late 1970s, after which the tracks were removed, although the station building survives as a holiday cottage. This sequence of photographs was taken at Craig-y-Nos during the filming of *Young Winston* (set during the Boer War) and depicts (left) the film's director, Richard Attenborough (now Lord Attenborough), striding along the platform, (facing page top) filming of the armoured train with Simon Ward (playing Young Winston) standing, bareheaded, in the first wagon and (facing page bottom) the Great Western Society's 0-4-2 tank No 1466 masquerading as a South African armour-plated tender engine. *Author-all*

'2251' class 0-6-0 No 2247 calls at Talybont-on-Usk with a Brecon-Newport train on 7 July 1962. Passenger services were withdrawn on 31 December 1962 and the station house is now Grade II Listed and used as a residential outdoor education centre. Various people, particularly school children who have stayed there overnight, believe the building to be haunted and that ghost trains pass by (despite the absence of track!). There have certainly been fatal railway accidents on this route, and the initials B&MR, which stand for the Brecon & Merthyr Tydfil Junction Railway Company, the original operator of the line, have been mischievously construed by some as standing for the Breakneck and Murder Railway! The problem was that Talybont stood at the foot of a 1 in 38 gradient known as the Seven Mile Bank which descended from Torpantau Tunnel (at 1310 ft above sea level, the highest standard gauge railway tunnel in Great Britain). On 2 December 1878, a runaway freight train hauled by two engines left the track at Talybont, killing members of the train crews, and on 3 February 1916 two freight trains collided on the other side of the summit between Torpantau and Pontsticill, again with some footplate men losing their lives. *Alan Sainty collection*

Pant Junction signalbox, seen on the right of this photograph, controlled the three lines which converged on Pant (not the Cambrian one): those to Brecon/Newport, Dowlais Central and Dowlais Top. Pannier tank No 9616 pauses at the station a few days before closure of the Brecon-Newport line on 31 December 1962. Pant marked the approximate boundary between the rural area to the north carrying mainly passenger traffic and the industrial south where mineral traffic to Newport Docks from the various ironworks and coal mines predominated. Part of the B&MR route is now covered by the narrow gauge Brecon Mountain Railway which operates a tourist service from its base at Pant northwards to Pontsticill and Dol-y-Gaer, and proposes to extend passenger services to Torpantau during 2013. The car park at Pant is built on the site of the Dowlais branch and on top of the ex- LNWR Morlais ('Miler') tunnel on the east/west route from Abergavenny and Rhymney Bridge to Merthyr, the final westerly section from Morlais Tunnel Junction through Pontsarn and Cefn Coed being a B&MR/ LNWR joint line. *R. W. A. Jones/Online Transport Archive*

With the platform gas lamps standing like silent sentinels against a bleak and freezing backdrop, No 9616 prepares to leave Brecon for Pant (see page 83) and eventually Newport. Originally, Brecon was served by four railway companies using three separate railway stations: the Brecon & Merthyr Tydfil Railway Co (B&MR) which arrived in 1863 and whose station was at Watton, the Mid Wales Railway (MWR, later absorbed by Cambrian Railways) from Llanidloes and also the Hereford, Hay & Brecon Railway (HH&BR), both arriving in 1864, their station being in Mount Street (the HH&BR was worked by the MWR until 1869 when the Midland Railway took over), and finally the Neath & Brecon Railway which reached Brecon in 1867, terminating at Free Street. In 1871, a new joint station was built at Free Street to replace all the others and, as can be seen from this photograph, it was a substantial edifice. This was partly to provide offices for all the railway companies. Brecon station closed to passengers on 31 December 1962, the Neath services already have been withdrawn on 15 October 1962. *R. W. A. Jones/Online Transport Archive*

Talyllyn station, on the former B&MR, was a junction at the entrance to a triangle. Trains from Brecon entered the station from a tunnel and either stopped at the main platform where the West Junction signalbox was located and opposite the station house/refreshment room or they used the former MWR/Cambrian Railways platform past the barrow crossing beyond the signalbox. This further platform, on which a pagoda hut stood, had no opposite platform. Instead it faced the junction with the Newport line (seen here diverging on the right). Trains using this further platform would not then be fouling the points for any following Newport train which would then proceed along the south eastern side of the triangle to Talyllyn East Junction. On leaving this further platform, trains would be on the north eastern side of the triangle and going via Talyllyn North Junction to Three Cocks Junction where they would either head for Llanidloes and Moat Lane Junction or Hay and Hereford. The third side of the triangle was north/south and used for trains avoiding Talyllyn station and travelling direct between South Wales and Mid Wales or Hereford. This picture depicts Ivatt Class 2 Mogul No 46522 in the process of leaving the north eastern side of the triangle with a Brecon-bound train and heading for the platform accessed from the main station building (now a private residence). The freezing passengers are waiting on the further platform for a Mid Wales or Hereford line service, the train already standing there presumably not going to their destination. *R. W. A. Jones/Online Transport Archive*

ABOVE This signpost was located on the main platform next to Talyllyn West Junction signalbox (seen on the left) and indicated which section of that platform (the main or the further part) passengers should use for particular destinations. The station seems to be doubling up as a pet cemetery. Under the bush behind the signpost are two grave stones in memory of Dick the blackbird (on the right) and Prince the dog (mostly obscured by the post). The 'Reserved for Staff' notice is presumably not marking their intended burial plot! *R. W. A. Jones/Online Transport Archive*

FACING PAGE BOTTOM AND RIGHT BR's last working steam locomotives were the three Swindon-built narrow gauge 2-6-2 tanks used on the Vale of Rheidol Railway (VOR) from 1923/4, when they were built, until the branch was acquired by a preservation group in 1989. The 11¾ mile line from Aberystwyth to Devil's Bridge opened in 1902 and was acquired by Cambrian Railways in 1913. These photographs depict: lower left, No 8 *Llywelyn* having its copper-capped chimney polished at the VOR shed at Aberystwyth on 22 July 1960 although whether the cleaner is appreciating the 13-year-old author taking his picture is uncertain; and this page, No 7 *Owain Glyndŵr* crossing the road as it pulls its train out of the former VOR station at Aberystwyth on 9 July 1960. The VOR was re-routed from its own terminus into the main station in 1968, occupying the bay platform vacated by Carmarthen trains when that line closed to passengers in 1964/5. *Author; Neil Davenport*

Dolgellau station (called Dolgelley until 12 September 1960) was a shared station (albeit with separate buildings) where the Cambrian Railways' branch from Barmouth Junction (renamed Morfa Mawddach on 13 March 1960) met end-on with the GWR's branch from Ruabon via Bala Junction, Corwen and Llangollen. This achieved the linking of the Cambrian coast with the GWR main line from Shrewsbury to Birkenhead. Initially, both lines into Dolgelley were run independently but in due course through services from Barmouth to Ruabon were operated and in this picture Mogul No 5330 is seen on 27 September 1962 bringing one such service into Dolgellau from Barmouth. Passenger services were withdrawn on 18 January 1965 but these had in any case been intermittent over various sections in the previous month due to flooding. Two parts of the original route have been reopened by preservation societies: the narrow gauge Bala Lake Railway which runs for 4^1/$_2$ miles between the original GWR station at Llanuwchllyn and Bala Lake Halt and the standard gauge Llangollen Railway which operates on 8^1/$_2$ miles of track between Llangollen and Carrog and hopes to reach Corwen shortly. *Alan Sainty collection*

ABOVE BR No 823 stands outside the Welshpool & Llanfair Light Railway shed at Welshpool shortly before the line closed to freight on 5 November 1956 (passenger services had been withdrawn on 9 February 1931). After the railway was closed, the two locomotives were fortuitously moved to Oswestry Works for storage (the author saw them there on 23 July 1960). Following the creation of a preservation society, No 822 was overhauled and returned to the line on 18 July 1961, hauling the first train on 4 April 1963. No 823 also returned and both locomotives are currently in service there. The railway was built primarily for the movement of agricultural produce, farm animals and timber either to the Montgomeryshire Canal in Welshpool or for transhipment by train, the W&L station being sited alongside the mainline station. The railway was constructed to a gauge of 2ft 6in, originally opening in 1903 (the engines were built in the previous year) and was acquired by Cambrian Railways. In recognition of the support provided to the railway by a local aristocrat, the Earl of Powis, the locomotives (Nos 1 and 2 in

pre-GWR days) were named *The Earl* and *The Countess*. When the GWR renumbered them, the nameplates were moved from the tank sides to the cab side sheets and No 823 had its name shortened to *Countess* to enable the plate to fit. Unlike the VOR locos, they never carried smokebox number plates. *Harry Luff/ Online Transport Archive*

BELOW Despite its abolition in 1922, Cambrian Railways was still lingering on at Wrexham on 21 July 1962! *Charles Firminger*

The sole surviving BR-built 'low bridge' '16XX' pannier tank, No 1638, now based on the Kent & East Sussex Railway, works a ballast train from Nantmawr quarry in summer 1964. The train, which is seen leaving Porthywaen and then crossing the A495 road at Porthywaen Crossing, is travelling along the former Cambrian Railways line between Blodwell Junction and Llynclys Junction heading for Oswestry in summer 1964. The line closed to freight in 1989 but was then mothballed, with the track remaining in place to the present day (but overlaid with tarmac at Porthywaen road crossing). Two preservation groups active in the area, The Tanat Valley Light Railway and Cambrian Heritage Railways, the latter based at the surviving station building at Oswestry, have already restored and operate sections of these lines, with the eventual aim of running trains from Gobowen through Oswestry and into the Tanat Valley. *John Collingwood/Online Transport Archive – both*

Oswestry station was the headquarters of Cambrian Railways on that company's main line from Whitchurch to Welshpool. Passenger services, which had started in 1864, were withdrawn on 18 January 1965 but the station remained open until withdrawal of the branch to Gobowen on 7 November 1966. This busy scene depicts No 7812 *Erlestoke Manor* on a Welshpool train. The station building on the Whitchurch platform to the left has been preserved and track reinstated for future heritage services.

No 7812 entered service in January 1939 and was withdrawn from Shrewsbury shed on 6 November 1965. Rescued from Barry scrapyard, the locomotive is based at the Severn Valley Railway. The station nameboard at Whitchurch, where Cambrian Railways connected with the LNWR, was particularly informative, as seen on 31 August 1957 against the backdrop of W5851W, a GWR corridor third of 1934 vintage. *Martin Jenkins/Online Transport Archive; Charles Firminger*

One of the benefits of the Oswestry to Whitchurch section of Cambrian Railways' main line was to regenerate Ellesmere which was losing ground to neighbouring towns with rail connections. Ellesmere station (in England) opened to passengers in 1863 and received a boost when a 12¾ mile cross-border line to Wrexham (in Wales) was opened in 1895, also operated by Cambrian Railways. Passenger services on the branch were withdrawn on 10 September 1962 but Ellesmere remained open to passengers until the former Cambrian main line, having been transferred from the WR to the LMR, was closed on 18 January

1965. This group of pictures shows (above) 0-4-2 tank No 1458 standing at Trench Halt with the 3.30pm from Wrexham Central to Ellesmere on 21 July 1962, The Trench being a district on the outskirts of Ellesmere; (facing page top) No 1458 again, on a misty day at Marchwiel; and (facing page top) No 1449 on arrival at Ellesmere with an elderly lady surprising the photographer by ignoring the prohibition sign and crossing the tracks instead of using the adjacent footbridge.
Charles Firminger; R. W. A. Jones/Online Transport Archive;
E. C. Bennett/Online Transport Archive

Apart from the Scottish Region's Dornoch branch on which two '16XX' pannier tanks were exiled, the most northerly destination for WR locomotives, albeit on an LMR line, was New Brighton on the tip of the Wirral facing Liverpool. Services had previously been run from Wrexham Central to Seacombe but from 4 January 1960, when Seacombe station closed to passengers, these services were diverted at Bidston to serve New Brighton instead. Latterly, DMUs normally operated the line but twice a year, on the Whitsun and August Bank Holidays, steam-hauled trains were provided, using rakes of five-coach non-corridor stock which were specifically retained for the purpose. These steam-hauled trains, using WR

pannier tanks or LMR 2-6-4 tanks due to restricted run round facilities at New Brighton, were referred to in the Supplement to the Working Timetable by the curious term 'diesel made steam'! Motive power was provided by the former WR shed at Wrexham called Croes Newydd (84J and later 89B, becoming 6C after transfer to the LMR in 1963). This group of photographs was taken on Whit Monday, 7 June 1965, the last year of steam operation, and depicts (above) No 9669 at Hawarden, (facing page top) No 4683 at Hope Village and (facing page bottom) No 9669 again at New Brighton, connecting with a Wirral Line electric service from Liverpool Lime Street. *Martin Jenkins/Online Transport Archive - all*

Index of locations

Aberbeeg 70
Abergwli 74
Abergywnfi 65
Aberystwyth 86, 87
Ashburton 23
Ashchurch 52

Backney Bridge 50
Ballingham 47
Barnstaple Junction 30
Beckford 53
Berkeley 38
Bewdley 56, 57
Blaenavon Low Level 71
Bowbridge Crossing Halt 41
Brecon 84
Bridgend 64
Brimscombe Bridge Halt 39

Cardigan 76
Carterton 13
Chalford 40
Chinnor 8
Clarbeston Road 75
Cleobury Mortimer 58
Coldharbour Halt 35
Colyton 19
Cowbridge 62
Cowley Bridge Junction 30
Craig-y-Nos 80, 81
Crumlin 69

Dolgellau 88
Downfield Crossing Halt 42
Dudley 54
Dulverton 31
Dymock 51

Easton 17
Edington Burtle 36
Ellesmere 93
Evesham (Midland) 53

Fairford 12
Fishguard Harbour 78
Furze Platt Halt 6

Hawarden 94
Heathfield 21, 22
Hemyock 34, 35
Hope Valley 95
Horspath Halt 9

Kilgerran 77
Kingswinford Junction 55

Lambourn 15
Lansallon 29
Lavernock 60
Lifton 24
Llanfair 89
Llanglydwen 77
Llantrisant 61
Looe 25
Lostwithiel 28
Luxulyan 27
Lydbrook Junction 43

Maesycwmmer 1
Marchwiel 93
Marlow 5
Melcombe Regis 17
Monks Risborough 7
Monmouth Troy 45, 46
Moretonhampstead 22

Nantymoel 64
Nelson & Llancaiach 73
New Brighton 95
Newbury 14, 15
Newent 51
Newquay 27

Oswestry 91

Standing at the Looe branch terminus at Liskeard, which still retains its GWR charm, steam railmotor No 93 makes history on 11 November 2012: a wooden-bodied vehicle originally built in 1908 carrying fare-paying passengers on the national rail network. *Frank Dumbleton*

Pant (Glam.) 83
Par 26
Penrhiwceiber 73
Pontsarn Halt 68
Porthcawl 63
Porthywaen 90
Princes Risborough 6
Princetown 24

Quakers Yard 71, 72

Rhoose 60
Ross-on-Wye 48, 49

St Ives 29
Sling 44
Staines 4
Strata Florida 79
Stroud 42

Taffs Well 66, 67

Talybont -on-Usk 82
Talyllyn Junction 85, 86
Tiverton 32, 33
Totnes 23
Towersey Halt 9
Treharris 72
Trench Halt 92

Upper Soudley 44

Wallingford 10, 11
Weymouth 16
Weymouth Quay 18
Whitchurch (Camb) 91
Wiveliscombe Front Cover
Wolverhampton Low Level 54
Wyre Forest 57

Yatton 37
Yeovil Town 20